The Colonies

The South Carolina Colony

Tamara L. Britton
ABDO Publishing Company

visit us at
www.abdopub.com

Published by ABDO Publishing Company, 4940 Viking Drive, Edina, Minnesota 55435.
Copyright © 2001 by Abdo Consulting Group, Inc. International copyrights reserved in all
countries. No part of this book may be reproduced in any form without written permission from
the publisher.

Printed in the United States.

Cover Photo Credit: North Wind Picture Archives
Interior Photo Credits: North Wind Picture Archives (pages 9, 11, 13, 15, 17, 19, 21, 25, 29);
    Corbis (pages 7, 23, 27)

Contributing Editors: Bob Italia, Kate A. Furlong, and Christine Fournier
Book Design and Graphics: Neil Klinepier

Library of Congress Cataloging-in-Publication Data

Britton, Tamara L., 1963-
    The South Carolina Colony / Tamara L. Britton.
        p. cm. -- (The colonies)
    Includes index.
    ISBN 1-57765-581-8
        1. South Carolina--History--Colonial period, ca. 1600-1775--Juvenile literature. [1.
South Carolina--History--Colonial period, ca. 1600-1775.] I. Title. II. Series.

    F272 .B73 2001
    975.7'02--dc21

                                                    2001022775

Contents

The South Carolina Colony

South Carolina is located along the Atlantic Ocean. Much of its soil is good for farming. Before the Europeans came, Native Americans called South Carolina home. The most powerful Native Americans were the Cherokee.

In the 1500s, the first Europeans came to South Carolina. In 1670, Captain Joseph West led a group of colonists to Port Royal. They began the first English settlement in South Carolina. They named it Charles Town, after King Charles II.

There were many rich men in South Carolina. There were also many poor people. In most families, women worked in the home. Men ran the government and worked the fields.

Farming was an important part of South Carolina's **economy**. Colonists built large plantations that grew rice, **indigo**, and cotton. The colony became successful.

England began to tax its colonies. But colonists thought the taxes were unfair. This led to the American Revolution.

The colonists won the war and founded the United States of America. On May 23, 1788, South Carolina **ratified** the U.S. **Constitution**. It became the eighth state of the new nation.

APPALACHIAN MOUNTAINS

BLUE RIDGE MOUNTAINS

▲ SASSAFRAS MOUNTAIN

CHEROKEE

The South Carolina Colony

NC

CATAWBA

ASHLEY RIVER

Charles Town (Charleston)

GA

YAMASEE

Charlesfort

Parris Island
Port Royal

ATLANTIC OCEAN

The Thirteen Colonies

NH

NY

MA

CT

RI

PA

NJ

MD

DE

VA

NC

SC

GA

ATLANTIC OCEAN

Detail Area

Early History

South Carolina is a state on the mid-Atlantic coastline. The Appalachian (ap-uh-LAY-shun) Mountains are in the west. A central **piedmont** region leads to a low, coastal plain in the east.

The coastal plain has many swamps. Its soil is good for farming. The piedmont region has claylike soil. The Blue Ridge mountain range is the highest land in South Carolina. Sassafras Mountain, at 3,560 feet (1,085 m), is the highest point in the state.

Many different Native American tribes lived in South Carolina. The Cherokee lived in the mountains in the northwest. They spoke the Iroquoian (ear-oh-KWOY-an) language. The Catawbas (kuh-TAOW-buhz) lived in the northeast and spoke the Souian (SOO-uhn) language. The Yamasee (YAH-muh-see) lived in the south. Their language was Muskhogean (muhs-KOH-ghee-uhn).

The Cherokee were the largest and most powerful Native Americans. They lived in homes made of poles covered with bark. Cherokee women grew corn, beans, and squash. The men hunted and fished.

Their tribe was divided into seven clans. The clans lived in many villages. Each village had two governments. The White Government ruled in times of peace. The Red Government ruled in times of war.

The sun sets on South Carolina's coast.

The First Explorers

In the 1520s, the first Europeans came to South Carolina. Explorer Giovanni da Verrazzano (gee-oh-VAH-nee dah ver-rah-ZAH-noh) sailed past South Carolina in 1524. Lucas Vásques de Ayllón (LOO-kass VAS-kays day eye-YON) of Spain explored South Carolina in 1526.

That year, Ayllón and about 500 people tried to start a colony in South Carolina. It was called San Miguel de Gualdape (sahn mee-GEL day gwahl-DAH-pay). But they lacked food. The winter was severe. Disease and Native American attacks killed many people. Ayllón was among those who died. Soon, the remaining colonists left.

In 1540, Spaniard Hernando de Soto explored South Carolina. He was searching for gold. In 1562, Frenchman Jean Ribault sailed up the South Carolina coast. He landed on Parris Island and started a colony there. It was called Charlesfort.

Ribault returned to France for more colonists and supplies. But Ribault did not return to Parris Island right away. The colonists were hungry. They needed food and supplies. So in 1563 they left.

Ribault's men build ships to carry them back to France.

Settlement

In 1629, England's King Charles I granted a **charter** to Robert Heath. The charter gave Heath all the land from Albemarle Sound to Florida. The charter called the land Carolana. But Heath never colonized the land.

In 1663, King Charles II owed money to eight men. They had helped him become king. So he renamed Heath's land Carolina. He gave it to the eight men. They became Carolina's **proprietors**.

That same year, Captain William Hilton explored South Carolina's land. He landed at Port Royal. In 1667, Captain Robert Sandford explored the land.

In March 1670, Captain Joseph West arrived at Port Royal Sound with about 100 colonists. They made the first English settlement on the Ashley River.

One year later, about 100 settlers came from Barbados. Soon many people wanted to come to Carolina for the religious freedom it offered.

In the late 1670s, the colonists decided to move the colony to a safer location. Gradually, the colonists moved to the **peninsula** on the Ashley River. The **proprietors** named the new settlement Charles Town, after King Charles II.

Charles Town before the American Revolution

Government

Carolina's **proprietors** created and filled all government offices. The most important office was the governor's. The proprietors also appointed a council, established courts, pardoned criminals, and collected taxes.

As soon as they arrived, the colonists organized a **militia** (muh-LISH-uh). They wanted to be able to protect themselves from the nearby Spaniards.

The proprietors asked John Locke to write a **constitution** for the colony. In 1669, he wrote the Fundamental Constitution. It made the colony a **feudal** society.

The colonists refused to adopt the constitution. But they did keep some of the constitution's laws. These laws included trial by jury and freedom of religion.

The colonists elected an assembly. Carolina's first elected assembly met in 1671. It created the colony's laws. But most Carolinians wanted more control over their government.

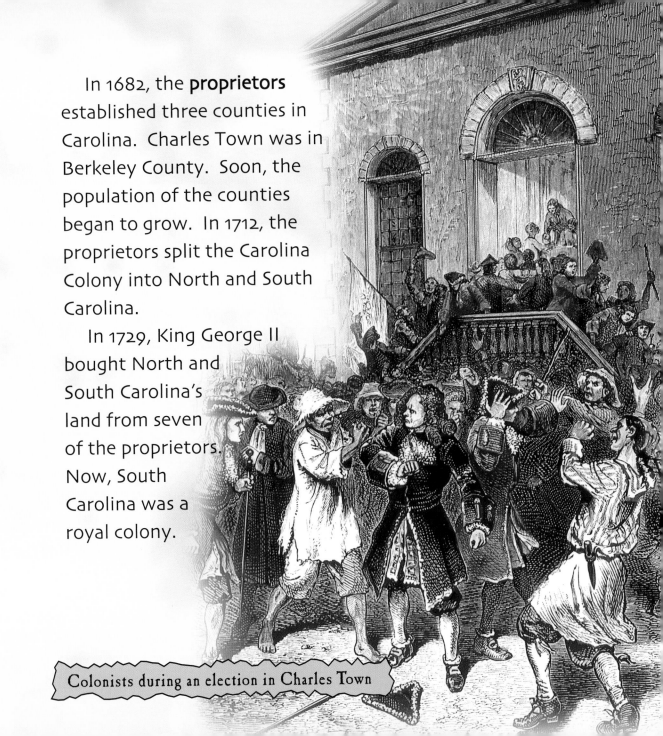

In 1682, the **proprietors** established three counties in Carolina. Charles Town was in Berkeley County. Soon, the population of the counties began to grow. In 1712, the proprietors split the Carolina Colony into North and South Carolina.

In 1729, King George II bought North and South Carolina's land from seven of the proprietors. Now, South Carolina was a royal colony.

Colonists during an election in Charles Town

Life in the Colony

South Carolina's society was divided into social classes. The upper-class people were merchants or planters. They worked little. They held dinner parties, danced, and went to horse races. Most of them owned slaves.

Upper-class women supervised the household. They were expected to know how to entertain guests. Some taught singing or embroidery lessons. Others **tutored** children in French, geography, or history.

The middle-class people were farmers, shipbuilders, tanners, carpenters, and shoemakers. They worked hard, hoping to become upper-class citizens. They also played pool, visited at inns, and participated in bearbaiting.

The lowest social class was made up of slaves. They did most of the labor in the colony. They were also skilled workers. Most of the carpenters, masons, and blacksmiths in Charles Town were slaves.

The Church of England was South Carolina's official church. But people of all faiths were welcome there. So there were Methodists, Huguenots (HEW-ga-notz), Quakers, Presbyterians (press-buh-TEER-e-unz), and other religious groups in the colony, too. South Carolina had one of the first groups of Jewish settlers in the 13 colonies.

Slaves relax outside their cabins on a South Carolina plantation.

Earning a Living

South Carolina's **economy** was based on farming. The coastal plain had good soil. The land was easy to clear. So many colonists built large plantations. The plantations grew rice, **indigo**, and cotton.

The most important crop was rice. Colonists built rice plantations along rivers and in swampland. Indigo was a difficult crop to grow. But the English paid high prices for it. Many planters bought slaves to work these crops.

The first slaves were brought to South Carolina from the West Indies in 1670. Many other slaves were brought from Africa. Slaves supported South Carolina's farming economy until the Thirteenth **Amendment** ended slavery in 1865.

South Carolina's manufactured goods included tar, **pitch**, and **turpentine**. They also made wood products such as shingles, planks, and barrels. Later colonists made linen and cotton cloth.

The colonists traded the goods they produced with other colonies, the West Indies, and England.

Colonists tend to a rice field in South Carolina.

Food

South Carolinians grew beans, squash, potatoes, and corn in their gardens. They also had plenty of rice. They raised livestock, so they enjoyed beef and pork.

The forests also provided foods for the colonists. Trees provided hickory nuts, black walnuts, and pecans. Persimmon and wild plum trees provided fresh fruit. There were also blackberries and cherries. Wild game such as deer, bear, turkey, and duck was abundant.

South Carolina's colonists ate much seafood. They enjoyed trout, shad, and sturgeon. They also enjoyed turtle meat and shrimp.

The water often made colonists sick. So South Carolinians made beer, ale, spirits, cider, and brandy. Upper-class colonists could afford to buy coffee, tea, and wine.

Women in the back country cooked over open fires. They cooked outdoors until they could build a cabin with a fireplace and a chimney. The colonists cooked their meals in iron or brass pots.

Colonists tend to their garden. They grew nearly all of their own food.

Clothing

Upper-class South Carolinians wore clothing from England. Women were known for wearing dresses of the latest fashion. Their dresses were made of rich fabrics called brocade and damask. They also wore dresses made of silk, lace, and velvet.

Men wore short pants called breeches, linen shirts, and tight-fitting jackets called doublets. Upper-class men's clothing was often as elaborate as women's. It was also made of fine fabrics from other countries.

Middle-class colonists made their own clothes. Women wore aprons, **bonnets**, and long dresses. Men wore breeches and doublets.

To make clothes, colonists grew cotton or flax, or raised sheep. The women spun the wool, flax, or cotton into thread on a spinning wheel. They wove the thread into cloth on a loom. Then they made clothes from the cloth.

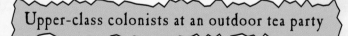

Upper-class colonists at an outdoor tea party

This practice became more popular with the upper class during the American Revolution. Women wove their own cloth in order to protest against buying England's fabrics.

Shelter

Early South Carolinians built their homes of clapboard and **tabby**. Their homes had one main room and a sleeping loft above. There was a fireplace on one end of the room. The fireplace provided a place for cooking, as well as a source of heat and light.

As colonists became successful, they built bigger houses. On the coastal plain, the climate was hot and humid. So wealthy colonists built houses with the rooms all in a row. These were called single houses.

The single house design allowed colonists to take advantage of cool summer breezes. The air could flow through windows on each side of the house and in each room. These homes also had a large porch called a piazza. It went along the length of the house.

Plantation owners often built double houses. They were two rooms wide. Each room had its own fireplace. These homes had many outbuildings for tasks such as cooking and washing laundry.

Elegant colonial houses in Charleston

Children

Education was important to upper-class South Carolinians. **Tutors** taught upper-class children at home. Then many of these children traveled to Europe to finish their education.

But lower-class parents needed their children to help on the farm. For about 50 years, South Carolina had no public schools. So these children did not have much formal education.

In 1710, the colony passed the Free School Act. In 1722, another act for free schools passed. Soon after, there were seven free schools in South Carolina. There were also many schools organized by religious groups, such as Anglicans or Presbyterians.

Some children did not attend school. At the age of six or seven, they became **apprentices**. Boys learned to be blacksmiths, coopers, tailors, and weavers. Girls learned to weave, spin, cook, and sew.

In rural South Carolina, children grew up on the farm. →

Slave children could not go to school. It was illegal to teach slaves to read or write. But some masters disobeyed the law and educated their slaves.

Native Americans

Many Native American tribes became the colonists' **allies**. But colonists continued to take Native American land.

For many years, the Cherokee got along with the colonists. They adopted colonial farming methods. Some Cherokee families had plantations. A few owned slaves.

The Catawba were enemies of the Cherokee. But they also became allies to the colonists. The colonists gave them guns to help them fight other tribes.

In the 1700s, the Yamasee moved from Florida to South Carolina. English merchants captured Yamasee and Catawba Native Americans and sold them into slavery.

In 1715, the Yamasee **rebelled**. They attacked Charles Town. But the next year, the Cherokee helped the colonists win the war. The Yamasee returned to Florida.

In 1756, England and France began to fight over America's land. This was called the French and Indian War. England sent troops to defend Charles Town. The Cherokee also fought for South Carolina. Other tribes fought for the French. England won the war in 1763.

Later, the U.S. government forced the Cherokee to leave their land. In 1838, U.S. troops led 14,000 Cherokee to a reservation in present-day Oklahoma. Many Cherokee died. This was called the Trail of Tears.

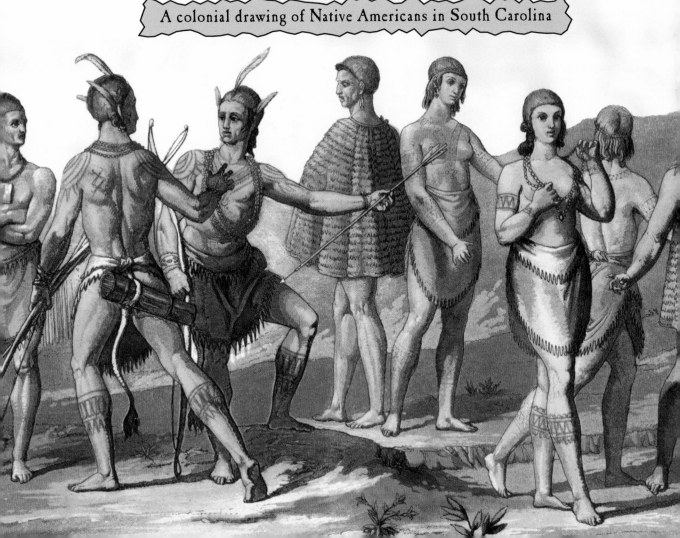

A colonial drawing of Native Americans in South Carolina

The Road to Statehood

The colonies needed help to protect themselves from attacks by Native Americans and European armies. So England sent troops to America to protect them. **Parliament** felt the colonists should pay for this protection. So Parliament passed laws to tax the colonists.

In 1765, Parliament passed the Stamp Act. It said that certain documents had to be taxed and receive a stamp to be legal. The colonists thought these taxes were unjust.

To protest, South Carolina sent five men to the **Continental** Congress in 1774. There, they declared independence from England. In 1775, the American Revolution began. The next year, South Carolina's assembly signed its first state **constitution**.

South Carolinians endured many battles. In June 1776, they defended Sullivan's Island against the English. But the English captured Charles Town in 1780. They occupied Charles Town until the end of the war.

Also in 1780, South Carolina's **militia** defeated the English at King's Mountain. They also had a victory at the

Battle of Cowpens in 1781. The colonists won the American Revolution in 1783.

On May 23, 1788, South Carolina **ratified** the U.S. **Constitution**. It became the eighth state of the new nation.

Today, South Carolina's **economy** is based mainly on manufacturing and trade. The state also grows cotton and tobacco. Each year, many people visit South Carolina's beaches, plantations, and historic battle sites.

The English invaded Charles Town during the American Revolution.

TIMELINE

1524 - Giovanni da Verrazzano sails past South Carolina

1526 - Lucas Vásques de Ayllón explores South Carolina; he starts a colony, which fails

1540 - Hernando de Soto explores South Carolina

1562 - Jean Ribault builds Charlesfort; colonists leave one year later

1629 - King Charles I grants a charter to Robert Heath for Carolana

1663 - King Charles II gives land to eight proprietors and calls it Carolina; William Hilton explores South Carolina

1667 - Robert Sandford explores South Carolina

1669 - John Locke writes Fundamental Constitution

1670 - Joseph West arrives at Port Royal Sound and begins a settlement, later called Charles Town; first slaves brought to Charles Town

1671 - Carolina's first assembly meets

1712 - North and South Carolina become separate colonies

1715 - Yamasee War begins; ends one year later

1729 - South Carolina becomes a royal colony

1756 - French and Indian War begins; ends seven years later

1765 - Parliament passes Stamp Act

1774 - Continental Congress meets; South Carolina declares independence from England

1775 - American Revolution begins; ends eight years later

1776 - Battle of Sullivan's Island

1780 - English capture Charles Town; Battle of King's Mountain

1781 - Battle of Cowpens

1788 - South Carolina becomes the eighth state in the United States of America

Glossary

ally - a nation that is linked to another by treaty.

Amendment - a change to the constitution of the United States.

apprentice - a person who learns a trade or craft from a skilled worker.

bonnet - a cloth or straw hat tied under the chin and worn by women and children.

charter - a written contract that states a colony's boundaries and form of government.

constitution - the laws that govern a state or country.

continental - of or having to do with the North American colonies.

economy - the way a colony or country uses its money, goods, and natural resources.

feudal - a ranked social system, where people had to pay in order to use the land.

indigo - a shrub with leaves that can be used to produce a deep blue dye.

militia - a group of citizens trained for war and other emergencies.

Parliament - England's lawmaking group.

peninsula - land almost completely surrounded by water but connected to a larger land mass.

piedmont - land lying at the base of the mountains.

pitch - a dark, sticky substance used for waterproofing and paving.

proprietor - one granted ownership of a colony, who is responsible for forming government and distributing land.

ratify - to officially approve.

rebel - to take up arms against a government.

tabby - a cement made of lime, sand, gravel, and oyster shells.

turpentine - a substance obtained from pine and fir trees.

tutor - a teacher who gives private lessons.

Web Sites

South Carolina Historical Society http://www.schistory.org
Click on Online Exhibits and learn about famous battles, favorite patriots, and old plantations in South Carolina.

African Americans in South Carolina http://www.sciway.net/afam/slavery/life.html
Learn about slaves' housing, culture, and daily life by reading first-hand accounts and viewing pictures of slave life in South Carolina.

These sites are subject to change. Go to your favorite search engine and type in South Carolina Colony for more sites.

Index